D1567534

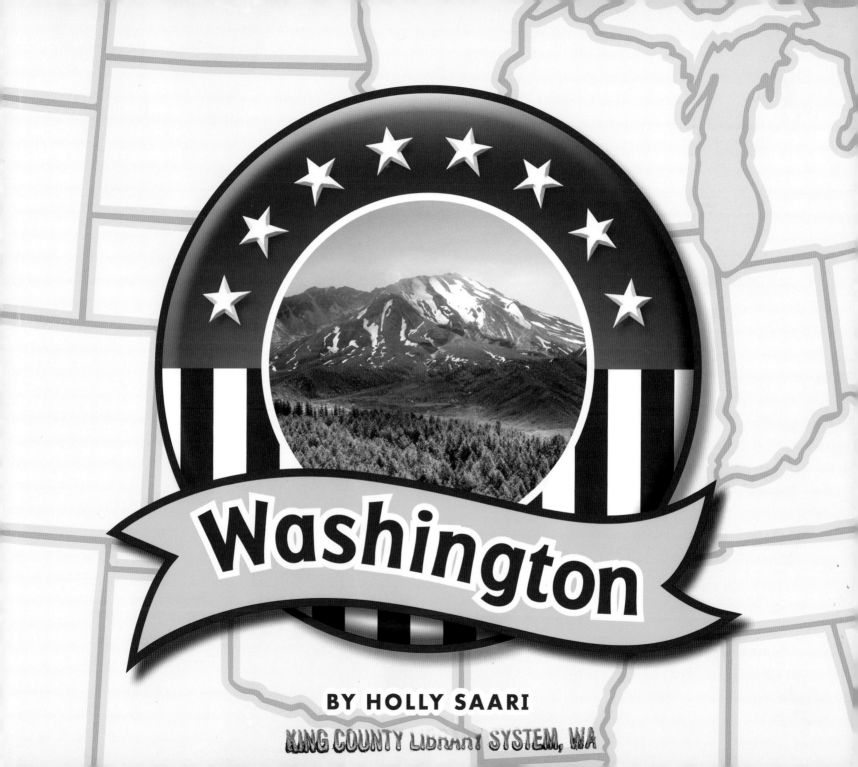

Washington

BY HOLLY SAARI

The Child's World

Published by The Child's World®
1980 Lookout Drive • Mankato, MN 56003-1705
800-599-READ • www.childsworld.com

ACKNOWLEDGMENTS
The Child's World®: Mary Berendes, Publishing Director
The Design Lab: Design and production
Red Line Editorial: Editorial direction

PHOTO CREDITS: Bill Perry/Shutterstock Images, cover, 1, 3; Matt Kania/Map
Hero, Inc., 4, 5; Jeremy Edwards/iStockphoto, 7; Jeff Hathaway/iStockphoto, 9;
123RF, 10; Bruce Kirk/Shutterstock Images, 11; Bruno Barbier/Photolibrary, 13;
North Wind Picture Archives/Photolibrary, 15; iStockphoto, 17; Matt Rourke/AP
Images, 19; Ted S. Warren/AP Images, 21; One Mile Up, 22; Quarter-dollar
coin image from the United States Mint, 22

LIBRARY OF CONGRESS CATALOGING-IN-PUBLICATION DATA
Saari, Holly.
  Washington / by Holly Saari.
    p. cm.
  Includes bibliographical references and index.
  ISBN 978-1-60253-492-6 (library bound : alk. paper)
  1. Washington (State)—Juvenile literature. I. Title.

F891.3.S23 2010
979.7—dc22
                                    2010019407

Printed in the United States of America in Mankato, Minnesota.
July 2010
F11538

On the cover:
Mount St. Helens is
part of Washington's
Cascade Mountains.

CONTENTS

Geography

Let's explore Washington! Washington is in the northwestern United States. Washington shares its northern border with Canada. The Pacific Ocean is to the west.

CANADA

Bellingham

WASHINGTON

Everett

Puget
Sound

Olympic
Mountains

Seattle

Spokane

Wenatchee

Tacoma

Ocean
Shores

Olympia ⭐

Cascade
Mountains

Ellensburg

Westport

Mount
Rainier

IDAHO

Mount Rainier
National Park

Lewis and
Clark Trail
State Park

Mount St.
Helens

Walla Walla

Pacific
Ocean

NORTH
WEST ● EAST
SOUTH

OREGON

5

Cities

Olympia is the capital of Washington.
Seattle is the largest city in the state.
Tacoma and Spokane are other large cities.

The Space Needle (center) is a famous place in Seattle. ▶

Land

Washington has the Olympic Mountains and the Cascade Mountains. The highest mountain in the state is Mount Rainier. Mount St. Helens is a **volcano** in Washington. The state also has low hills and flat coasts. Puget Sound is a large **inlet** in western Washington.

Many people enjoy nature in Mount Rainier National Park. ▶

Plants and Animals

Washington has many forests. It is nicknamed "the **Evergreen** State." The state tree is the western hemlock. The state bird is the willow goldfinch. It has yellow feathers. The state flower is the coast rhododendron. It often has pink **petals**.

The coast rhododendron was chosen as the Washington state flower in 1892. ▶

People and Work

About 6.5 million people live in Washington. Most people live in cities. **Logging**, fishing, and farming are important jobs in the state. Apples, wheat, pears, and cherries are important Washington products. Many paper products are made here, too. Jobs in **technology** are also important. These include making airplanes and computers. Some people work in **tourism** jobs.

Workers pack apples at a fruit-packing company. ▶

Two large companies have main offices in Washington. Microsoft Corporation is a large computer company. Amazon.com, Inc., is an Internet superstore.

History

Native Americans have lived in this area for thousands of years. People from Europe first explored the area in the late 1700s. In the 1800s, England and the United States argued over who owned the area. In 1848, the area of Washington became a part of a **territory** of the United States. On November 11, 1889, Washington became the forty-second state.

Settlers built towns in the Washington area in the 1800s. ▶

Washington is named after George Washington, the first president of the United States. Washington is the only state named after a president.

Ways of Life

Outdoor activities are **popular** in Washington. Many people ski, fish, boat, and camp. Art and science **museums** can be found in some of Washington's large cities. Music is important in Washington, too. The state is also known for its many coffee shops, especially in Seattle.

Many people enjoy water activities on Puget Sound. ▶

Famous People

Musicians Bing Crosby, Jimi Hendrix, and Kurt Cobain were born in Washington. Bill Gates was also born here. He is one of the founders of Microsoft.

Bill Gates was born in Seattle. He cofounded Microsoft in 1975. ▶

Famous Places

The Pike Place Fish Market in Seattle is a popular place to visit. Workers here put on a show by throwing fish to each other. The Lewis and Clark Trail State Park is in Washington. It is a great place to explore nature.

Meriwether Lewis and William Clark explored the Washington area in 1806.

The Pike Place Fish Market holds fish-throwing contests. ▶

State Symbols

Seal

A picture of first U.S. President George Washington is on Washington's state seal. Go to childsworld.com/links for a link to Washington's state Web site, where you can get a firsthand look at the state seal.

Flag

The green background of Washington's flag stands for the state's forests.

Quarter

Mount Rainier is on Washington's state quarter. The quarter came out in 2007.

Glossary

evergreen (EV-ur-green): An evergreen is a tree that does not lose its leaves. Washington is called "the Evergreen State."

inlet (IN-let): An inlet is a narrow body of water that cuts into an area of land from a larger body of water. Puget Sound is an inlet in Washington.

logging (LOGG-ing): Logging is cutting down trees to use for lumber or other wood products. Logging is an important industry in Washington.

museums (myoo-ZEE-umz): Museums are places where people go to see art, history, or science displays. Museums are in some of Washington's largest cities.

petals (PET-ulz): Petals are the colorful parts of flowers. The rhododendron, Washington's state flower, often has pink petals.

popular (POP-yuh-lur): To be popular is to be enjoyed by many people. Music, art, and outdoor activities are popular in Washington.

seal (SEEL): A seal is a symbol a state uses for government business. A picture of George Washington is on Washington's state seal.

symbols (SIM-bulz): Symbols are pictures or things that stand for something else. The seal and the flag are Washington's symbols.

technology (tek-NAWL-uh-jee): Technology is scientific knowledge applied to practical things. Some people in Washington have jobs in the technology field.

territory (TAYR-uh-tor-ee): A territory is a piece of land that is controlled by another country. Washington was part of a territory of the United States.

tourism (TOOR-ih-zum): Tourism is visiting another place (such as a state or country) for fun or the jobs that help these visitors. Because many visitors come to Washington, many people work in tourism.

volcano (vol-KAY-no): A volcano is a place in the ground, often on top of a mountain, from which lava, steam, and ashes shoot. Mount St. Helens is a famous volcano in Washington.

Further Information

Books

Keller, Laurie. *The Scrambled States of America*. New York: Henry Holt, 2002.

Smith, Marie, and Roland Smith. *E is for Evergreen: A Washington Alphabet*. Chelsea, MI: Sleeping Bear Press, 2004.

Thornton, Brian. *The Everything Kids' States Book: Wind Your Way Across Our Great Nation*. Avon, MA: Adams Media, 2007.

Web Sites

Visit our Web site for links about Washington: *childsworld.com/links*

Note to Parents, Teachers, and Librarians: We routinely verify our Web links to make sure they are safe and active sites. So encourage your readers to check them out!

Index